CELEBRATIONS

Chris Deshpande
Photographs by Zul Mukhida

Contents

About this book 2

Mardi gras 4
Make a papier-mâché maraca

Easter 6
Decorate hard-boiled eggs

Eid ul-Fitr 8
Make printed greetings cards

Holi 10
Make a flower garland

The Dragon Boat Festival 12
Make a concertina paper dragon

Raksha Bandhan 14
Make plaited bracelets

Harvest 16
Make salt dough models

Chanukkah 18
Decorate candles

Birthdays 20
Make woven God's Eyes

All Souls' Day 22
Make sugar icing skulls

Diwali 24
Make clay candle holders

Christmas 26
Make an Advent curiosity box

New Year 28
Make paper-cut lanterns

More things to find out about 30

Where to find out more 31

Index 32

A&C Black · London

About this book

What's your favourite day of the year? Perhaps it's your birthday or a festival day, such as Christmas, Diwali, Chanukkah or Holi. This book is about festivals and how they are celebrated around the world. It shows you how to make craft objects associated with festivals and gives you plenty of ideas to help you design your own craft objects.

This book will tell you about stories, traditions and crafts which are based on festivals. At the back of the book, there is information on how to find out more about these crafts and traditions, with details about places to visit and books to read.

Some of the craft activities in this book are more complicated than others and will take longer to finish. It might be fun to ask some friends to help with these activities, for example making the Advent curiosity box on page 26.

Before you start working on any of the craft projects, read through the instructions carefully. Each step-by-step instruction has a number. Look for the same number in the picture to see what each stage of your model should look like.

Before you begin

Collect together everything listed in the 'you will need box'.

Ask an adult's permission if you are going to use a sharp tool, dye cloth or use an oven.

Prepare a clear work surface.

If the activity is going to be messy, cover the surface with old newspaper or a waterproof sheet.

Mardi gras

Mardi Gras is carnival time. At the famous Mardi Gras carnival in Rio de Janeiro, Brazil, there are parties, feasts and parades in the streets. These celebrations mark the beginning of Lent, which is the time when Christians remember the story of Jesus's fast in the wilderness.

Mardi Gras is also known as Fat Tuesday because people used to eat up any eggs, fat and butter in the house before giving them up for Lent. In England, pancakes are eaten, and the day is known as Pancake Day or Shrove Tuesday.

At Mardi Gras there are colourful processions, with people having as much fun as possible before Lent. There is music, singing and dancing, and people wear amazing masks and costumes.

Try to make a papier-mâché maraca to shake at carnival time. In the Caribbean, maracas are made from hollow gourds, which are big fruits, filled with beads.

You will need: newspaper torn into pieces, a small bowl of wallpaper paste without fungicide, an old roll of sticky tape, a glue brush, a balloon, dried chick peas, a piece of thin cardboard for the handle (about 9cm square), paints, brushes and varnish.

1 Blow up the balloon, but don't make it too big. Rest the knotted end in the middle of an old roll of sticky tape so that it is easy to work on. Gently brush wallpaper paste all over the balloon. Dip a piece of paper into the paste and then place on to the balloon. Continue to cover the balloon with pasted paper, overlapping the pieces slightly to make a smooth surface. Cover the balloon with about four layers of paper.

2 To make the handle, roll the cardboard into a narrow tube and tape together. Attach to the balloon by pasting long strips of paper to the handle and half-way up the balloon. Strengthen the join round the neck of the balloon with strips of paper which run the other way. Cover the balloon with paste and leave to dry for about two days.

3 Pop the balloon with a needle. Put a handful of chickpeas into the hollow maraca. Block up the handle with some scrunched-up newspaper. Cover with papier-mâché to seal the end. Leave to dry. Paint and varnish your maraca.

Easter

Easter is a Christian festival which is celebrated around the world. It remembers the story of Jesus's return from the dead. On Good Friday, Jesus died on the cross. In Germany, this day is known as Silent Friday because no church bells are rung. On Easter Sunday, Jesus rose from the dead.

The word Easter comes from the name of the ancient goddess of spring, who was called 'Eostre'. Many Easter customs are based on the springtime flowering of plants and birth of animals. Often at Easter, chocolate and decorated eggs are given as presents, because eggs are a symbol of new life.

Here are some ways to decorate hard-boiled eggs. Try to make up some of your own as well. **Ask an adult to help you hard-boil the eggs.** Make sure the eggs are cold before you start to decorate them. Remember these eggs are for decoration only.

In Poland wax designs are painted on to eggs. This kind of design is called batik. Try making your own batik eggs.

1 Draw your design on to the egg with a wax crayon. Place the egg in a bowl of vegetable dye, made from either cold tea or the water left over from boiling up spinach or beetroot. Or you could mix 1 tablespoon of turmeric with a cup of hot water. Leave the egg in the dye for 30 minutes.

2 Draw a pattern with wax crayon on to an egg and colour the spaces in-between with poster paint.

3 Cut shapes from tissue paper and paste on to the egg with PVA.

4 Eggs can be painted with poster paint or inks and left plain. They can be varnished with PVA or decorated with coloured paper.

5 **Ask an adult to help you hard-boil an egg.** Carefully drain it on a slatted spoon. While the egg is still hot, pick it up with an old towel. Crayon all over the egg with a wax crayon. The heat of the egg melts the crayon and makes a smooth coating of wax. When the egg is cool, scratch a design into the wax coating with a needle.

Eid ul-Fitr

Eid ul-Fitr is an important festival in the Islamic calendar, which comes at the end of a month-long fast called Ramadan. During Ramadan, Muslims do not eat or drink anything from dawn until after sunset.

Eid ul-Fitr is a happy time when people go to parties, buy new clothes and give each other presents and cards. The Muslim religion forbids the drawing of people or animals, so Eid cards are decorated with beautiful designs made from geometric patterns.

Try designing your own geometric patterns and printing your own cards or wrapping paper. To find some ideas for your patterns look at pictures of Islamic buildings, such as the Dome of the Rock in Jerusalem, below.

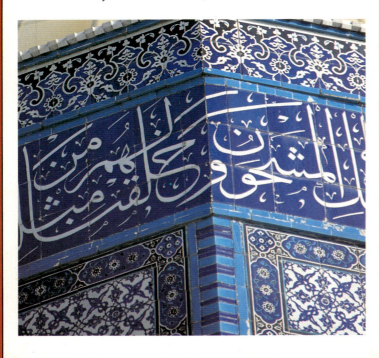

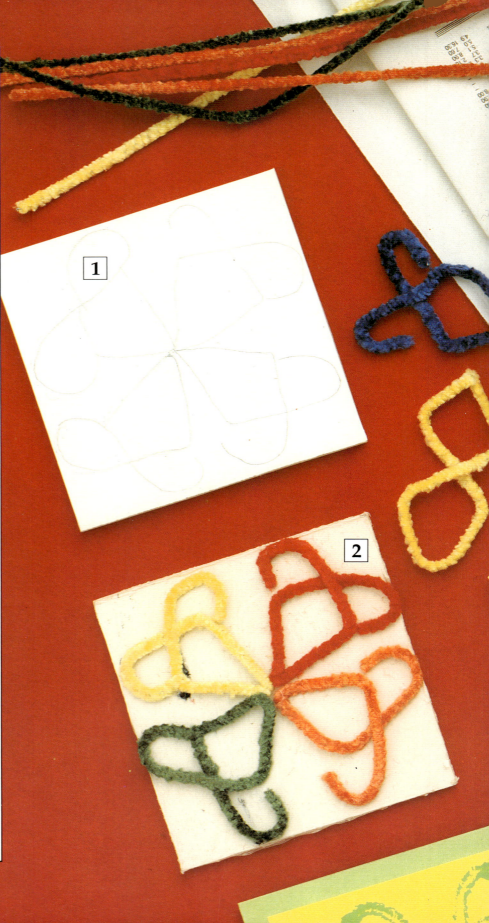

You will need: cardboard (the back of a cereal packet), scissors, pencil, pipe-cleaners, glue brush, glue, a paint brush or a small paint roller, paints, paper.

1 Cut an 8cm square of cardboard. On the square, make a rough pencil sketch of the pattern you want to print. Bend and twist the pipe-cleaners into shapes which can be made into this pattern.

2 Apply a thin layer of glue to the cardboard square. While it is still wet, press the pipe-cleaner shapes into place and leave to dry.

3 Use a paint brush or roller to apply paint to the raised pattern on your printing block. Place the block on top of the paper and gently smooth over the surface with your hands.

4 Carefully pull away the block to see the printed pattern.

Try printing some wrapping paper. You could use a number of different patterns or repeat one pattern. Try printing a border for writing paper with small printing blocks.

Holi

Holi is a Hindu festival held in the spring. It is celebrated mostly in India. It's a time of games and pranks when people remember the stories of Lord Krishna and the tricks and jokes he played. For three to five days, there are processions, and people sing and dance in the streets. Today, part of the fun is to squirt coloured water and paint on to your friends and neighbours.

Make a splatter painting

> **You will need: old newspaper, an old sponge, water, paints, paint brushes, paper.**

Splatter painting can be messy, so before you begin, put down lots of old newspaper. Use the sponge to dampen a clean sheet of paper, but be careful not to make the paper too wet. Use a paint brush to flick and drip paint on to the paper, or take a pinch of powder paint and drop it on to the paper. Watch the patterns form as the paint runs.

Holi is also a festival which celebrates the arrival of spring and the blossoming of spring flowers.

Make a paper flower garland

You will need: scissors, a roll of crêpe paper, stem wire, a thick needle, thread.

1 To make one flower, cut an 8cm wide strip from the folded roll of crêpe paper.

2 Unroll this strip and roll it up again loosely into a cylinder shape, crunching the paper as you go. Bind wire round the middle of the paper. Tuck in any sharp pieces of wire or cover them with sticky binding tape.

3 On either side of the wire, open out the crêpe paper into petals. Make lots of flowers in this way.

4 To make a garland, use a big needle and thread to sew the flowers together.

Look at different flowers and see if you can make paper ones which look similar. Try to make paper daffodils and roses.

The Dragon Boat Festival

At the Chinese Dragon Boat Festival, races are held in brightly coloured boats, which are decorated with dragons' heads and tails. Everybody makes a lot of noise and splashes the water.

Many people believe that the festival is based on the story of a poet called Qu Yuan who lived in ancient China. Qu Yuan thought that the rulers of the day were cruel and unfair, so he decided to drown himself in protest. He threw himself into the middle of the river. All the villagers raced their boats across the river to try to save him but they were too late. The poet drowned. The villagers were worried that the fish in the lake would eat the poet's body so they made lots of noise to frighten the fish away.

Make a paper dragon

You will need: two very long strips of paper (about 75cm × 2.5cm), cardboard, glue, round-ended scissors, a pencil, coloured felt tips, foil, sequins.

1 Make the dragon's body with two strips of paper. Glue the ends of the strips together at right angles, as in the picture.

2 First, fold the bottom strip over the top strip, and then fold the top strip over the bottom strip. Continue until you have a concertina of paper. Glue the ends together.

3 Draw and cut out a dragon's head. You can decorate it with coloured felt tips, coloured card, foil, and sequins.

4 Stick the dragon's head to one end of the dragon's body. Make a paper tail by curling long triangular strips of paper round the end of a pair of rounded scissors. Glue these to the other end of the dragon.

Raksha Bandhan

Raksha Bandhan is a festival celebrated by most Hindu and Sikh families. It's a day when families remind each other of how much they love one another. On this day, a sister ties a plaited bracelet, called a rakhi, around her brother's wrist, and he promises to look after her.

There are many stories about Raksha Bandhan. Here is a Hindu story. Indra, who was the King of the Gods, lost his heavenly kingdom in a war with the demon King Bali. Indra's wife prayed for help. Then Lord Vishnu gave her an amulet, or lucky charm, which he told her to fix around Indra's wrist. The amulet protected Indra in battle, and good was seen to triumph over evil.

You can make plaited rakhis from long strips of fabric, string, ribbon or wool. You will need strips of fabric or thread which are roughly two-and-a-half times the length of the plait you want to make. Here's how to make a three-strand rakhi with ribbon.

Knot the ends of the ribbon together. It may help to pin the ribbon to a cork board. Move the threads over each other as shown. When you have moved each ribbon once, repeat the moves. To finish the plait, knot the ends of the ribbon together.

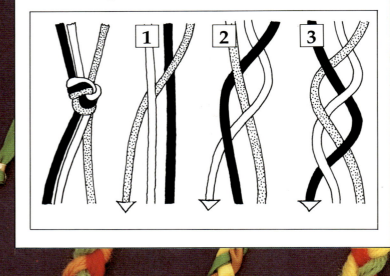

Try making a five-strand rakhi from thick wool. This plait is made in two steps which are repeated. It will help if you use five different coloured wools.

Knot the ends of the wool together. First, the far right thread is taken over the next two threads to the centre. Then the far left thread goes over the next two threads, to the centre. After five steps the order of the threads is reversed. After ten steps the threads are back in place. To finish, knot the ends of the threads together.

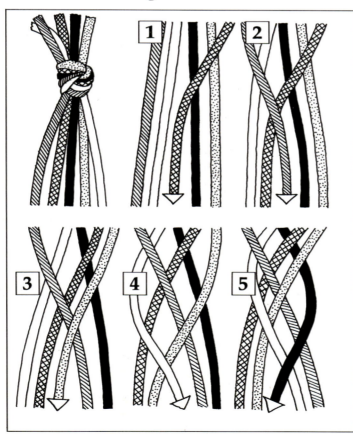

Decorate a disc of card with tinsel, foil and sequins. Stitch the disc of card to the middle of the plaited band, with the bead or button at the centre.

You could give your rakhi to a friend.

Harvest

All over the world, people celebrate the gathering of the harvest. After the hard work of planting and tending to the crops all year, harvest is a time of happiness and thanksgiving.

In Punjab in India, villagers perform a very energetic dance called Bhangra, which acts out the sowing, tending and reaping of the crops.

Long ago, in England, the last of the corn from the harvest was kept and twisted into the shape of a person, a sheaf of wheat or a cross. These shapes became known as corn dollies. The dolly was kept through the winter and sown with new corn the next spring. The corn spirit was then 'saved and kept alive' until the following spring.

Make some harvest models from salt dough

You will need: 325g plain flour, 225g salt, 250ml water, 1 tablespoon of oil, a wooden spoon, a bowl, natural food colouring, paints, varnish, paint brush, baking tray, greaseproof paper, an oven set to Gas mark 2 (300°F or 150°C).

Mix the flour and salt together. Then add the water and oil. Shake some flour over your hands and knead the mixture into a dough.

Use a small piece of dough and model it into the shape of a harvest corn dolly. Try making models of your favourite harvest fruit and vegetables.

You can colour the salt dough before you cook it with natural food colouring. Add a few drops of colouring to the dough. Knead in the colour to make it even. Or you can cook your salt dough shape first and then paint and varnish it afterwards.

Put your models on to a baking tray lined with greaseproof paper. **Ask an adult to help you put it in the oven.** Bake for about one and a quarter hours, until the models are hard.

Chanukkah

Chanukkah is the Jewish festival of light. It is based on the following ancient story. A Syrian emperor forbade the Jews from praying in their Temple in Jerusalem. Eventually the Jews won back the Temple, but there was only enough oil for the eternal light for one day. Miraculously, the oil lasted eight days. This is why Chanukkah lasts for eight days.

The Chanukkiyah is a candlestick with nine holders. It holds a candle for each day of the festival and a servant candle which is used to light the others. The Chanukkiyah stands for light, truth and the triumph of good over evil.

The oldest Jewish symbol is a seven-branched candlestick called a menorah. Each branch symbolises one of the days of creation.

Decorate a candle

You will need: a long candle, the stub from an old coloured non-flammable wax candle, a small saucepan, an old ring pull lid can, a wooden spoon, an old wooden chopping board or cork mat resting on plenty of newspaper, a kettle, a gas ring.

1 **Ask an adult to help you to prepare the hot wax.** Put the stub of an old coloured candle into the can. Stand the can in the saucepan. Boil some water in the kettle and pour about 4cm into the bottom of the saucepan. Gently heat the saucepan, until the wax starts to melt.

Ask an adult to help you remove the saucepan from the heat. Place the saucepan on an old wooden chopping board.

2 Hold the unused candle over the can and use the spoon to dribble coloured wax over it. Allow the wax to harden.

19

Birthdays

What special things do you do on your birthday to remember the day on which you were born? All over the world, people celebrate birthdays with parties and presents. In South America, children are given 'God's Eyes' on their birthdays. These are sticks fastened into a cross and woven with coloured wool. Each different colour of wool stands for a year of the child's life.

You can make tiny God's Eyes from cocktail sticks or bigger ones from bamboo canes and lolly sticks.

You will need: cocktail sticks or short bamboo canes, sewing cotton, scissors, lengths of different coloured wool or strips of fabric, glue, beads.

1 Find the middle of each stick. Bind the middle of the sticks together with cotton. First, wrap the cotton round the sticks diagonally one way, and then the other. Make sure the sticks are securely joined. Tie the two ends of the cotton together and cut just beneath the knot.

2 Glue the end of one of the colours of wool to the centre. Wrap the wool over and under each arm in turn.

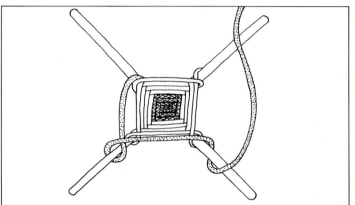

When you want to finish one colour, glue the wool firmly round one arm and cut away any spare wool.

To start a new colour, glue the wool around this same arm. Then continue to wrap the wool in a figure of eight.

3 Try gluing beads on the ends of the arms of your God's Eyes. Or make tassels which hang from the arms.

Can you think of a way of joining a number of God's Eyes together?

All Souls' Day

All Souls' Day is a day when the Christian Church remembers all those people who have died. Some people believe that on the night of All Souls' Day (November 2nd) the souls, or spirits, of dead people visit their old homes. Some people place lanterns and candles in their windows to guide the spirits to food and drink which has been prepared for them inside. In Mexico, some families make an altar in their homes for dead relatives. They decorate the altar with marigolds and icing sugar skulls.

Try making some icing sugar skulls

You will need: ready-made fondant icing, icing sugar, a spoon, a chopstick, a chopping board, natural food colouring.

Divide the fondant into small balls which fit inside your palm. If the fondant becomes sticky, it may help to dust your hands with icing sugar.

You can make the skulls either hollow or solid. Try modelling the balls of fondant with the end of a spoon and a chopstick. Give the skulls deep eye sockets and teeth. Smooth the skulls with your fingertips.

Try making some skulls from different coloured fondant. Before you begin to shape each skull, add a few drops of colouring to the fondant. Gently knead the colouring into the icing so that it is evenly spread. Or you can paint the finished skulls different colours with food colouring.

Diwali

Diwali is an important Hindu celebration, known as the festival of light. It is also a New Year festival. Diwali remembers the story of Prince Rama and his wife Sita, who were banished from their home for fourteen years. They had many adventures and eventually were guided back home by villagers who lit small lamps called divas.

At Diwali time, divas are lit in memory of this story and to attract Lakshmi, the goddess of health and prosperity, to homes.

Sikhs also celebrate at Diwali time. They remember the story of the release of the sixth Guru Hargobind Singh from the Moghul Emperor's prison. Try to find out more about the stories behind Diwali.

Make a clay diva

You will need: an old chopping board, a rolling pin, self-hardening clay, a modelling tool, non-flammable paint, a paint brush, a night light candle with a metal base.

1 Roll out the clay so that it is about 1cm thick. Mark out a leaf shape big enough to take the night light candle. Cut round this shape with the tool, leaving an extra 1cm to spare.

2 Shape the diva in your hand so that it has a slightly raised edge and tapers at one end. You can prick a pattern into the clay with the tool.

3 Leave it to dry. Decorate your diva with painted patterns.

4 Place the night light candle in the diva and **ask an adult to light it**. Candles can be dangerous: never lean over a lit candle or leave it unattended in a room. Always blow out candles when you have finished with them.

Christmas

Christmas is the time when the Christian Church celebrates the story of the birth of Jesus. The month leading up to Christmas is known as Advent, which means the 'coming'. Some churches have Advent wreaths, which are circles of woven holly, with holders for four candles. Holly, which is evergreen, symbolises new life, and the candles symbolise Jesus as the light of the world. On each Sunday leading up to Christmas, a candle is lit. This custom comes from Scandinavia.

Often Advent calendars are given to children as presents. The calendars have twenty-five windows, which open out to show pictures. On each day leading up to Christmas, a window is opened. On Christmas morning, the last window is opened.

Advent calendars are fun and easy to make. Try to make one which can hold small presents.

You will need: 25 empty matchboxes, which are all the same size, elastic bands, cardboard, scissors, felt tip pens, paints, a paint brush, strong glue, 25 paper fasteners, coloured paper, sequins.

1 Paint the drawers of the boxes. For the handles, make a hole in the middle of the front of each drawer and push in a paper fastener. Open out the arms of the paper fasteners at the back, to hold them in place.

Put each drawer back in its shell.

2 Before you glue your boxes into columns, think about how you want your Advent calendar to look. Each column could be the same height or you could make an Advent calendar with columns of different heights, similar to the one in the picture. When you've decided, glue the boxes on top of each other. To help the boxes stay in place while they dry, place an elastic band around them.

3 When each column has dried, glue the columns next to each other. Number the drawers from one to twenty-five.

4 Cut the cardboard to cover the top and sides of the big box and glue on.

Decorate your Advent box with paper shapes and sequins.

Make tiny presents to put inside each box. What will you put inside box number twenty-five, which is opened on Christmas morning?

27

New Year

Many religions have their own calendars, which means that people celebrate New Year at different times. The Sikhs celebrate their New Year, Baisaikhi, in April. The Hindus celebrate their New Year, Diwali, in late October or early November. The Jewish New Year Festival called Rosh Hashanah happens in September or October.

In some parts of the world New Year's Day is always on January 1st. But many people use lunar calendars, which are arranged according to the phases of the moon so New Year's Day changes its date each year.

Each New Year festival has its own traditions and customs. The Chinese name each year after one of twelve different animals. To celebrate New Year, they make huge dancing lions and decorate the streets with lanterns.

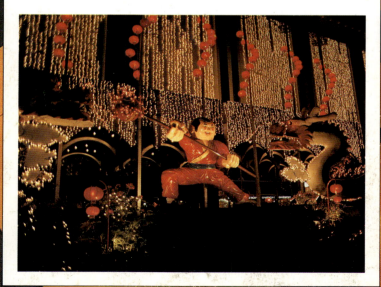

Try making some paper lanterns, with paper which has been folded, cut and scored into interesting patterns. Here are a few suggestions of ways to cut your paper. Try to make up some of your own as well.

> **You will need: a flat work surface covered with lots of newspaper, paper, a craft knife, a pencil, a ruler, round-ended scissors, sticky tape, cotton thread.**

Ask an adult to help you use the craft knife.

1 Cut long triangular strips from the paper. Gently curl them round a pair of round-ended scissors. Can you make paper rolls from any other shapes?

28

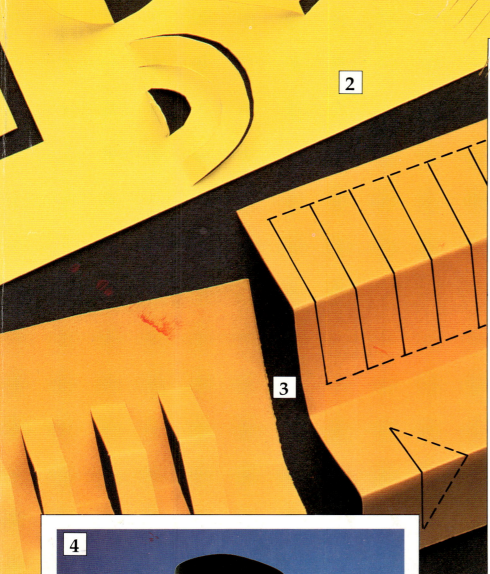

[2] On the paper, draw an even number of half shapes which fit inside each other. Carefully cut round each line. Fold back every other strip of paper. Experiment with different shapes, including triangles, circles and squares.

[3] Take a piece of paper and fold or pleat it a number of times. Press on each fold firmly.

Use a ruler to draw squares and half-triangles on the centre of each fold. Draw solid lines which run up and down the sides of the shapes. Draw dots for lines at the top and bottom of each shape.

Put a ruler on the dotted lines and score along them with a craft knife. Use the knife and ruler to cut along the solid lines. Push out the shapes from the fold.

[4] When you have made paper cuts all over your piece of paper, stick the sides of the paper together to make a lantern. Fix some thread to the top of the lantern. Hang it by a window so that light can shine through it.

More things to think about

This book shows you how to make and model papier-mâché and salt dough, cut and fold paper and plait thread. You can use these different craft techniques to make your own craft objects based on festivals.

Many festival days are a time of remembering happy or sad events or old stories. Sometimes the stories are religious. To get some ideas for making your own craft objects, find out as much as you can about the story behind a festival.

As you find out more about a particular story, you will see that certain signs and symbols have come to stand for the festival, for example the diva for Diwali, or the menorah for Chunakkah. Some festivals share similar symbols, such as light, or the growth of plants and animals in spring. Can you think of your own symbols for certain festivals? Think about how you could use festival symbols in your craft design.

Visit museums and ask old people in the community how festivals used to be celebrated in the past. Make sketches of any interesting decorations or symbols. Two hundred years ago, Christmas was celebrated very differently from the way it is celebrated today. Try to find out when Christmas trees first became popular.

Think of all the different ways that festivals can be celebrated. There may be parties, where people wear traditional clothes and eat specially prepared food. Do you and your family have any special customs for festival days? Can you include any of these ideas in your craft project?

Find out how people in different parts of the world celebrate the same festival, for example harvest festival. Try to find out about harvest customs, traditions and legends in China, India and Italy.

Your craft object could be a present, decoration, greetings card, or a musical instrument. Think about the best craft technique to use, for example you could model salt dough or papier-mâché, or cut and fold paper. Do you want the finished object to be flat or three-dimensional? Do you want it to have moving parts or to hang from the wall? When you have answered these and similar questions, think carefully about the best way of making your craft object and the best materials to use.

Experiment with different kinds of decoration for your craft object. How could you include symbols as decoration? Think about all the ways you can create different textures, colours and shades with paper, cloth or by modelling papier-mâché. Try making one huge and one tiny version of your craft object, for example you could make an enormous Advent curiosity box, or a tiny flower garland to wear as a bracelet.

How to find out more

Information books about festivals and religions

Christmas Tim Wood (A&C Black)
A look at Christmas at the turn of the century, with photographs, objects and documents.

* **My belief** (Franklin Watts)
An introduction to different religions as seen through the eyes of young people.

* **Our culture** Jenny Wood (Franklin Watts)
Customs and traditions of different cultures, including Hindu, Sikh, Muslim and Rastafarian.

* **Celebrations** (A&C Black)
How major festivals are celebrated at home and school.

Books about crafts and technology

* **Fresh start** (Franklin Watts)
A step-by-step approach to different craft media. Titles include **Clay**, **Fabric art**, **Papier mâché**, **Masks**, **Paper crafts** and **Jewellery crafts**.

* **Arts and crafts** (Wayland)
A clear step-by-step approach to crafts with ideas for developing designs. Titles include **Batik and tie-dye**, **Block printing** and **Weaving**.

* **Toybox science** Chris Ollerenshaw and Pat Triggs (A&C Black)
Scientific principles explained through toys. A helpful guide to making working models.

* **Make it work** Peter Firmin (A&C Black)
How to build working models from rubbish, including the technology of pulleys, levers and winches.

* indicates a series rather than one book.

Places to visit

The following list gives a selection of places to visit which have major collections of objects from around the world. Don't forget to look in your local town or city museum too.

Commonwealth Institute
230 Kensington High Street, London W8
Each country in the commonwealth has its own display of art and crafts.

Horniman Museum
100 London Road, London SE23
A collection showing arts, crafts and religions of the world.

Pitt Rivers Museum
South Parks Road, Oxford OX1 3PP
Lieutenant General Pitt Rivers, born in 1827, collected a wide range of objects from countries all over the world which he visited as a soldier.

Victoria and Albert Museum
Cromwell Road, London SW7
A vast collection of nineteenth century artefacts.

Index

Advent 26
Advent calendar 26–27, 30
All Souls' Day 22

Bhangra 16
birthdays 20
Brazil 4

candles 18–19
Caribbean 4
Chanukkah 18–19, 30
Chinese festivals 12, 28
Christian festivals 4, 6, 22, 26
Christmas 26
corn dollies 16

decorating
   candles 19
   eggs 6–7
divas 24, 30
Diwali 24, 28, 30
Dragon boat festival 12

Easter 6
eggs 6–7
Eid ul-Fitr 8
England 4, 16

festivals of light 18, 24, 28, 30

God's eye 20
Good Friday 6
Guru Hargobind Singh 24

harvest 16
Hindu festivals 10, 11, 14, 24, 28
Holi 10–11
holly 26

icing sugar skulls 22
India 10, 16
Indra 14
Islamic calendar 8

Jesus 4, 6, 26
Jewish festivals 18, ·28

King Bali 14

Lakshmi 24
Lent 4
Lord Krishna 10
Lord Vishnu 14
lunar calendars 28

Mardi gras 4
menorah 19, 30
Mexico 22
modelling
   clay divas 25
   icing sugar skulls 23
   salt dough 17
Muslim festivals 8

New Year 28

painting
   hard-boiled eggs 6
   splatter painting 10
pancake day 4
paper crafts
   paper-cut lanterns 28
   paper dragon 13
   paper flower garland 11
   papier-mâché maraca 4–5
plaiting
   rakhis 14–15
Prince Rama 24
printing
   Eid cards 8–9

Qu Yuan 12

rakhi 14
Raksha Bandhan 14
Ramadan 8

salt dough 16–17
Scandinavia 26
Sikh festivals 14, 24, 28
Sita 24
South America 20
spring 6, 10, 11, 16
symbol 18, 26, 30

weaving
   God's Eyes 20–21

First published 1993
A & C Black (Publishers) Limited
35 Bedford Row, London WC1R 4JH

Reprinted 1995

ISBN 0 7136 3714 5
© 1993 A & C Black (Publishers)
Limited

A CIP catalogue record for this book
is available from the British Library.

Acknowledgements
Line drawings by Barbara Pegg
Photographs by Zul Mukhida, except
for: p4, p8, p28 Life File Photographic
Agency; p12 Robert Harding
Photographic Agency; p18 Jewish
Education Bureau.

With grateful thanks to Langford and
Hill Limited, London, for supplying
all art materials.

Craft objects made by Tracy Brunt
except for those on p6–7, which were
made by Dorothy Moir.

All rights reserved. No part of this
publication may be reproduced in any
form or by any means – graphic,
electronic or mechanical, including
photocopying, recording, taping or
information storage and retrieval
systems – without the prior
permission in writing of the
publishers.

Filmset by Rowland Phototypesetting
Limited, Bury St Edmunds, Suffolk
Printed in Italy by L.E.G.O.